PROSPERING IN PANDEMONIUM

RELEASING AND RESTORING
THE DOUBLE PORTION

STUDY GUIDE

Copyright © 2022 by Jeremiah Hosford

Published by Arrows & Stones

All rights reserved. No portion of this book may be reproduced, stored in a retrieval system, or transmitted in any form or by any means—electronic, mechanical, photocopy, recording, scanning, or other—except for brief quotations in critical reviews or articles, without prior written permission of the author.

Unless otherwise noted, all scripture quotations marked **NKJV** are taken from the New King James Version®. Copyright © 1982 by Thomas Nelson. Used by permission. All rights reserved. | Scripture quotations marked **KJV** are taken from the King James Version of the Bible. Public domain. | Scripture quotations marked **TPT** are from The Passion Translation®. Copyright © 2017, 2018 by Passion & Fire Ministries, Inc. Used by permission. All rights reserved. ThePassionTranslation.com.

For foreign and subsidiary rights, contact the author.

Cover design by: germancreative
Cover Photo by: Creative Focus Studios

ISBN: 978-1-957369-47-1   1 2 3 4 5 6 7 8 9 10

Printed in the United States of America

PROSPERING IN PANDEMONIUM

RELEASING AND RESTORING
THE DOUBLE PORTION

STUDY GUIDE

JEREMIAH HOSFORD
───── FOREWORDS BY ─────
PAT SCHATZLINE & DR. FRANCIS MYLES

CONTENTS

Chapter 1. The Prophetic vs. Pandemonium 6

Chapter 2. Revelation Revealed and Released 10

Chapter 3. Here vs. There 14

Chapter 4. The Return and the Reward 18

Chapter 5. The Enemy Within 22

Chapter 6. The Purpose of Position 26

Chapter 7. The Sound of the Time, The Time of the Sound .. 30

Chapter 8. More Than Conquerors 34

Chapter 9. The Vicarious Savior 38

Chapter 10. The Double Portion Dimension 44

Chapter 11. The Wealth Transfer 48

Chapter 12. The Beginning of His End 52

PROSPERING IN PANDEMONIUM

RELEASING AND RESTORING THE DOUBLE PORTION

STUDY GUIDE

JEREMIAH HOSFORD

FOREWORDS BY
PAT SCHATZLINE & DR. FRANCIS MYLES

CHAPTER 1

THE PROPHETIC VS. PANDEMONIUM

"The real battle is not the storm that is raging or the pandemonium surrounding you. The real battle is deciding which one you will choose to believe—what you see with your natural eyes or what you hear with your spiritual ears."

READING TIME

As you read Chapter 1: "The Prophetic vs. Pandemonium" in *Prospering in Pandemonium*, reflect on the questions and scriptures.

REFLECT AND TAKE ACTION:

Throughout God's Word, when does He usually send a prophetic word to His people?

_____
_____
_____
_____
_____
_____
_____

Why do you think God sends people to prophesy? What is the purpose of prophecy?

_____
_____
_____
_____
_____
_____
_____

What is a double portion? What would a double portion look like in your life?

_____
_____
_____
_____
_____
_____
_____

> **2 Chronicles 20:20b (KJV)**
>
> *"Believe in the Lord your God, so shall ye be established; believe his prophets, so shall ye prosper."*

Consider the scripture above and answer the following questions:

What does this verse say awaits those who trust in the Lord and His prophets?

_____
_____
_____
_____
_____
_____
_____
_____
_____

What do you think prevents people from trusting in God and His prophets as the above verse says to do? Have you ever been guilty of this?

_____
_____
_____
_____
_____
_____
_____
_____
_____

Do you think that all the "delays" we experience in life are from the enemy? Does God ever send a delay? If so, why?

_____
_____
_____
_____
_____

What do you think oftentimes stands in the way of us believing God-sent prophecy about the future?

_____
_____
_____
_____
_____

How can we guard against the deception of the enemy?

_____
_____
_____
_____
_____

How can we be delivered from the fear that comes along with pandemonium?

_____
_____
_____
_____
_____

CHAPTER 2

REVELATION REVEALED AND RELEASED

"Revelation is the difference-maker . . . It is the difference between someone who has knowledge of the double portion and someone who walks in the double portion."

READING TIME

As you read Chapter 2: "Revelation Revealed and Released" in Prospering in Pandemonium, reflect on the questions and scriptures.

REFLECT AND TAKE ACTION:

In your own words, what is revelation and heavenly revelation?

_____
_____
_____
_____
_____
_____

Is there any area of your life that you're settling for less in? What is it?

_____
_____
_____
_____
_____
_____

What's one piece of revelation you've received in the past year? Have you applied this revelation to your day-to-day thinking and living?

_____
_____
_____
_____
_____
_____

> *Zechariah 9:12 (NKJV)*
>
> *"Return to the stronghold, you prisoners of hope. Even today I declare that I will restore double to you."*

Consider the scripture above and answer the following questions:

What do you think is meant by the "double" spoken about in this verse?

_____
_____
_____
_____
_____

What does this verse say is first required before one has double restored to them?

_____
_____
_____
_____
_____

What are the mediums for God to give us revelation? Can we find revelation through the lives of others?

_____
_____
_____
_____

What does it mean to walk in the double portion? Is this the same as having knowledge of the double portion? Are you walking in the double portion?

_____
_____
_____
_____
_____
_____

How does one go about obtaining the double portion?

_____
_____
_____
_____
_____

Do you think it's possible for us to miss the heavenly revelation God intends us to learn and apply? Why or why not?

_____
_____
_____
_____
_____

CHAPTER 3

HERE VS. THERE

"He is releasing the double portion! He's releasing such a move of His Spirit that you will not be able to count—or even estimate—the number of people that it will impact."

READING TIME

As you read Chapter 3: "Here vs. There" in Prospering in Pandemonium, reflect on the questions and scriptures.

REFLECT AND TAKE ACTION:

How does Satan cloud our perception of the work and goodness of God? Has he ever done this to you?

_____
_____
_____
_____
_____

What does the author mean when he states that there was a war between his "here and there"? Have you experienced this battle in your own life?

_____
_____
_____
_____
_____

If God promises something to you, do you trust in it wholeheartedly? Are you ever swayed or made unsure by your current circumstances?

_____
_____
_____
_____
_____

> **Psalm 73:1-3 (NKJV)**
>
> *"Truly God is good to Israel, to such as are pure in heart. But as for me, my feet had almost stumbled; my steps had nearly slipped. For I was envious of the boastful, when I saw the prosperity of the wicked."*

Consider the scripture above and answer the following questions:

What caused the author of this psalm (Asaph) to "almost slip" as he mentions?

_____
_____
_____
_____
_____

Have you ever been envious of the money, prestige, power, or achievements of the wicked?

_____
_____
_____
_____
_____

Do you ever have trouble humbling yourself? Do you think God is waiting for you to approach Him humbly to release His promises into your life?

_____
_____
_____
_____

Have you ever attributed your earthly troubles and pain to coming from the Lord Himself? If so, describe the experience.

_____
_____
_____
_____

Has God ever used one of your perceived "setbacks" in life as a setup to propel you forward and upward? Explain.

_____
_____
_____
_____

What is radical obedience? Would you describe yourself as a radically obedient Christian? Why or why not?

_____
_____
_____
_____

Have you ever received a "right-now word" from the Lord? If so, what was it?

_____
_____
_____
_____

CHAPTER 4

THE RETURN AND THE REWARD

"The anointing of God is not released through fear. It's released through faith!"

READING TIME

As you read Chapter 4: "The Return and the Reward" in *Prospering in Pandemonium*, reflect on the questions and scriptures.

REFLECT AND TAKE ACTION:

What is the difference between a demonic stronghold and a kingdom stronghold? Which is more powerful?

_____
_____
_____
_____
_____
_____

In your own words, what is the "Spirit of Anti-Anointing" that the author describes in this chapter?

_____
_____
_____
_____
_____
_____

What do you feel is currently keeping the church from returning to the full anointing God intended?

_____
_____
_____
_____
_____
_____

> **Hebrews 11:6 (NKJV)**
>
> *"But without faith it is impossible to please Him, for he who comes to God must believe that He is, and that He is a rewarder of those who diligently seek Him."*

Consider the scripture above and answer the following questions:

Why is faith required to please the Lord? What does it look like to live and operate in faith?

_____
_____
_____
_____
_____

What does it mean to diligently seek the Lord? How do you think He rewards those who diligently seek Him?

_____
_____
_____
_____
_____

Which of the 10 listed items on page 65 do you feel you personally need to work on the most? Which do you feel the church needs to work on the most as a whole?

_____
_____
_____
_____

What areas of your life is the anointing of God being blocked by the enemy?

Are you fearful in any areas of your life? If so, what are they?

How do you think the world will look if all of God's children fully return to His anointing?

CHAPTER 5

THE ENEMY WITHIN

"The greatest opposition to walking in the double-portion anointing does not come from without but from within."

READING TIME

As you read Chapter 5: "The Enemy Within" in *Prospering in Pandemonium*, reflect on the questions and scriptures.

REFLECT AND TAKE ACTION:

Have you ever stood in the way of something God has wanted to do in or through you? Why?

_____
_____
_____
_____
_____
_____

What happens when we walk in the flesh instead of walking in faith?

_____
_____
_____
_____
_____
_____

Do you think there's room for both God's Word and the mind of the flesh in our life? Why or why not?

_____
_____
_____
_____
_____
_____

> **1 Corinthians 2:14 (NKJV)**
>
> *"But the natural man does not receive the things of the Spirit of God, for they are foolishness to him; nor can he know them, because they are spiritually discerned."*

Consider the scripture above and answer the following questions:

What do you think this verse means when it talks about the "natural man"?

_____
_____
_____
_____
_____
_____

What will it take for someone to receive and understand the things of the Spirit of God?

_____
_____
_____
_____
_____
_____

Would you say you're more focused on a timeline, or the finish line? Explain.

_____
_____
_____

What does the author mean when he states, "Walking in the flesh causes us to reap a harvest of corruption"?

Why can't one who is walking in the flesh discern and understand things of the Spirit? How can they change this?

Why do you think God doesn't always give us a time line? Do you think this can aid us in the long run?

CHAPTER 6

THE PURPOSE OF POSITION

"There is a purpose for obeying the Lord when it comes to the alignment of our will with the kingdom of God in order to receive what He has for us."

READING TIME

As you read Chapter 6: "The Purpose of Position" in *Prospering in Pandemonium*, reflect on the questions and scriptures.

REFLECT AND TAKE ACTION:

In your own words, why is positioning so important?

_____
_____
_____
_____
_____
_____

Has disobedience to the Lord ever caused you to be out of position for a blessing? If so, explain the circumstance.

_____
_____
_____
_____
_____
_____

Do you feel you're currently positioned to receive the promises, progress, and protection of God? If not, what needs to change?

_____
_____
_____
_____
_____
_____

> *Malachi 3:10-11 (NKJV)*
>
> *"'Bring all the tithes into the storehouse, that there may be food in My house, and try Me now in this,' says the Lord of hosts, 'If I will not open for you the windows of heaven and pour out for you such blessing that there will not be room enough to receive it. And I will rebuke the devourer for your sakes, so that he will not destroy the fruit of your ground, nor shall the vine fail to bear fruit for you in the field,' says the Lord of hosts; . . ."*

Consider the scripture above and answer the following questions:

What is the meaning of the above verse? What does it reveal about how God operates?

_____
_____
_____
_____
_____
_____
_____

Do you think the Lord would follow through with His promise even if the Jewish people were disobedient to His commands? Why or why not?

_____
_____
_____
_____
_____
_____

What seeds of your life need attention? Where do you need to grow?

_____
_____
_____
_____
_____

Do you think the double portion is achievable without proper positioning? Why or why not?

_____
_____
_____
_____
_____

Does disobedience change the fact that God wants to bless us? What is the true danger of disobedience?

_____
_____
_____
_____
_____

Does positioning just have to do with location and faith? What else does it include?

_____
_____
_____
_____
_____

CHAPTER 7

THE SOUND OF THE TIME, THE TIME OF THE SOUND

"There are giftings and capacities within this generation that God, in His sovereignty, saw and said this generation has what it takes to advance during this time. YOU WERE BORN FOR NOW!"

READING TIME

As you read Chapter 7: "The Sound of the Time, The Time of the Sound" in *Prospering in Pandemonium*, reflect on the questions and scriptures.

REFLECT AND TAKE ACTION:

Do you trust that God has plans for you, specifically in the here and now?

_____
_____
_____
_____
_____

What do you think the church of America and of the world needs to do to gain ground and operate in the double portion God intended?

_____
_____
_____
_____
_____

Do you think God gave you giftings that specifically for the here and now? What are they?

_____
_____
_____
_____
_____
_____

> **Romans 8:28 (NKJV)**
> *"And we know that all things work together for good to those who love God, to those who are the called according to His purpose."*

Consider the scripture above and answer the following questions:

How has God used negative circumstances in your life for good?

_____
_____
_____
_____
_____
_____
_____
_____
_____
_____

Do you think God is using the circumstances occurring in the world right now for the good of His people as well?

_____
_____
_____
_____
_____
_____
_____
_____

What happens when we get distracted by what is going on around us instead of focusing on what is happening in us?

How has the enemy succeeded in distracting you from God's will?

What gifting(s) do you feel God has entrusted to you for the advancement of His kingdom?

CHAPTER 8

MORE THAN CONQUERORS

"When we fight from a place of victory, we must realize that just because we are not man's choice does not mean we're not God's choice."

READING TIME

As you read Chapter 8: "More Than Conquerors" in *Prospering in Pandemonium*, reflect on the questions and scriptures.

REFLECT AND TAKE ACTION:

Why is it important to understand we must fight from a place of victory and should not fight for a place of victory?

_____
_____
_____
_____
_____
_____

Do you think worship and praise is important in the life of a believer? Why or why not?

_____
_____
_____
_____
_____
_____

What/who in this chapter does the author equate to being God's bow and arrow?

_____
_____
_____
_____
_____
_____

> *Romans 8:37 (NKJV)*
>
> *"Yet in all these things we are more than conquerors through Him who loved us."*

Consider the scripture above and answer the following questions:

What do you think it means to be "more than conquerors" as the above verse states?

_____
_____
_____
_____
_____
_____

Can we achieve this level of victory by our own strength?

_____
_____
_____
_____
_____

Have you ever tried to fight for a place of victory instead of from one? What was the outcome?

_____
_____
_____
_____
_____

Do you think praise is an essential ingredient in victory? Why is praise so powerful?

___

What areas of your life is God adding to you?

___

Do you think God can use anyone to combat the kingdom of darkness? Who is excluded from this?

___

CHAPTER 9

THE VICARIOUS SAVIOR

"When Jesus walked this earth, He walked in the double-portion anointing. When we allow Him to live His life through us daily, He is bringing the double-portion anointing with Him."

READING TIME

As you read Chapter 9: "The Vicarious Savior" in *Prospering in Pandemonium*, reflect on the questions and scriptures.

REFLECT AND TAKE ACTION:

Do you believe Jesus wants to live through you? What would this look like in your day-to-day life?

_____
_____
_____
_____
_____
_____

What words, phrases, or principles do you feel culture has highjacked from the kingdom of God?

_____
_____
_____
_____
_____
_____

If Jesus Himself was running your business, your family, or had your general responsibilities, what do you think He would do differently?

_____
_____
_____
_____
_____
_____

> **Romans 8:10 (TPT)**
>
> *"Now Christ lives his life in you! And even though your body may be dead because of the effects of sin, his life-giving Spirit imparts life to you because you are fully accepted by God."*

Consider the scripture above and answer the following questions:

What do you think this verse means when it says, ". . . Christ lives his life in you! And even though your body may be dead because of the effects of sin . . ."?

_____
_____
_____
_____
_____
_____
_____
_____

What does it mean for Christ to live His life in us? Do you think this should affect the entirety of our lives, or just some areas?

_____
_____
_____
_____
_____
_____
_____
_____

Do you ever feel like you're facing the enemy and his attacks alone? Explain.

_____
_____
_____
_____
_____
_____
_____

How do you think the culture of the church and the world would change if all believers lived as if Jesus was living through them?

_____
_____
_____
_____
_____
_____
_____

If Jesus was walking the earth today and you were one of His disciples, how would you respond in the face of adversity? What is stopping you from responding like this today?

_____

_____

_____

_____

_____

Take time to list three areas of your life you want to radically shift to live more like Jesus. What are some tangible objectives you can list below to make these a reality?

1) _____

Objectives: _____

_____

_____

2) _____

Objectives: _____

_____

_____

3) _____

Objectives: _____

_____

_____

CHAPTER 10

THE DOUBLE PORTION DIMENSION

"Walk in this dimension! Minister in this dimension! Parent in this dimension! Run your business in this dimension! Live in this dimension! By faith, it is yours!"

READING TIME

As you read Chapter 10: "The Double Portion Dimension" in *Prospering in Pandemonium*, reflect on the questions and scriptures.

REFLECT AND TAKE ACTION:

In your own words, what does the author mean when he states that the double portion is not a season, but a dimension?

_____
_____
_____
_____
_____
_____

Is living in the double portion anointing a new concept? Did people live in this anointing during biblical times?

_____
_____
_____
_____
_____
_____

What does the author mean when he discusses "immediately moments" in this chapter?

_____
_____
_____
_____
_____
_____

> *John 17:22-23 (NKJV)*
>
> *"And the glory which You gave Me I have given them, that they may be one just as We are one: I in them, and You in Me; that they may be made perfect in one, and that the world may know that You have sent Me, and have loved them as You have loved Me."*

Consider the scripture above and answer the following questions:

How does the fact that Jesus has given us the glory bestowed upon Him by the Father change your thinking?

_____
_____
_____
_____
_____
_____

What areas of your life are you not living with Christ's glory in?

_____
_____
_____
_____
_____

In what ways do you need to change to live and think how Jesus intended you to?

_____
_____
_____

In what ways has your culture and environment clouded and limited your perception of God and your identity?

Are there any areas of your life that you are not living within the double portion dimension? What are they?

CHAPTER 11

THE WEALTH TRANSFER

"It is time for the church to pick our head up and get ready because He is about to avenge His people and take the wealth of the wicked and transfer it into the hands of the righteous."

READING TIME

As you read Chapter 11: "The Wealth Transfer" in *Prospering in Pandemonium*, reflect on the questions and scriptures.

REFLECT AND TAKE ACTION:

Will God ever allow enemies to attack us? What is the purpose of this?

_____
_____
_____
_____
_____
_____

Do you think being bombarded by the attacks of enemies can actually benefit us? If so, how?

_____
_____
_____
_____
_____
_____

Of the biblical examples provided in this chapter that discuss God's people and their enemies, which sticks out to you and why?

_____
_____
_____
_____
_____
_____

> ***Proverbs 13:22 (NKJV)***
>
> *"A good man leaves an inheritance to his children's children, but the wealth of the sinner is stored up for the righteous."*

Consider the scripture above and answer the following questions:

What does the above verse reveal about wealth transfer?

_____
_____
_____
_____
_____
_____

Do you think that, in this verse, the words "inheritance" and "wealth" only speak of money?

_____
_____
_____
_____
_____
_____

What do we need to do to position ourselves to hear the Spirit of God?

_____
_____
_____
_____

Has God revealed any revelation to you recently? If so, what was it?

_____
_____
_____
_____
_____

Do you think your giving and your prosperity are correlated in any way? Why or why not?

_____
_____
_____
_____
_____

What areas of your life are you trusting in others more than in God?

_____
_____
_____
_____
_____

What do you feel is preventing you from receiving the double portion?

_____
_____
_____
_____
_____

CHAPTER 12

THE BEGINNING OF HIS END

"Just when the devil thinks it's over, God has just begun. It's the beginning of his end."

READING TIME

As you read Chapter 12: "The Beginning of His End" in Prospering in Pandemonium, *reflect on the questions and scriptures.*

REFLECT AND TAKE ACTION:

In your own words, what is the double portion? Compare your answer to your initial answer in Chapter 1 of this study guide.

_____
_____
_____
_____
_____

Do you believe God wants to grant you a double portion?

_____
_____
_____
_____
_____

As a child of God, what does the wealth transfer Jesus won through His death look like for your life?

_____
_____
_____
_____
_____

> **2 Corinthians 8:9 (NKJV)**
>
> *"For you know the grace of our Lord Jesus Christ, that though He was rich, yet for your sakes He became poor, that you through His poverty might become rich."*

Consider the scripture above and answer the following questions:

What does this verse mean when it says that we might be rich through Christ becoming poor?

_____
_____
_____
_____
_____
_____
_____
_____
_____

Do you feel you live as though you were made rich through Christ becoming poor?

_____
_____
_____
_____
_____
_____
_____
_____
_____

How should your thinking and the way you live change once you recognize Satan has been defeated and disarmed?

_____
_____
_____
_____

What areas of your life need to change for you to live fully in the double portion anointing?

_____
_____
_____
_____

Take time to think and list areas of your life that you're waiting for the floodgates of heaven to open upon and be intentional to share them with others:

1) _____

2) _____

3) _____

4) _____

5) _____

6) _____

www.ingramcontent.com/pod-product-compliance
Lightning Source LLC
Chambersburg PA
CBHW062123080426
42734CB00012B/2972